REMAKING AMERICA IS UP TO YOU!

The Future Is Outside the Box

Before designing the future we must learn from the past and understand the present!

by

George Lopac Jr.

DORRANCE
PUBLISHING CO
EST. 1920
PITTSBURGH, PENNSYLVANIA 15238

Dorrance Publishing Co
585 Alpha Drive
Suite 103
Pittsburgh, PA 15238
Visit our website at *www.dorrancebookstore.com*

ISBN: 978-1-6453-0221-6
eISBN: 978-1-6453-0847-8

PREFACE

DRACULA FEARS SUNLIGHT.

WOLF MAN FEARS A FULL MOON.

FRANKENSTEIN FEARS FIRE.

POLITICIANS FEAR VOTES.

Summary

America is a crippled republic! The country is in a state of *common-sense confusion* and *civic ignorance.* Too many people do not know how their government works or how it should work. Too many people have given up on the democratic process: low voter turnouts and an indifferent attitude toward the legislative process. Throughout the country, common sense is not common practice because *we do not understand the essence of common sense.* These two weaknesses form a "perfect storm" for the dark side of politics to manipulate the democratic process for the benefit of political parties and special-interest groups. The attitude in Congress is party before country and people. The remaking of America will require elimination of the "perfect storm." The new paradigms developed address that issue. Implementation of the new paradigms has two prerequisites.

▶ Change our indifferent attitude toward the democratic process into an aggressive, proactive participation. *We must know who and what we are voting for at all levels of government.*

▶ Create a national awareness of the true essence of common sense: barriers, supports, and the power as a tool for decision-making and problem-solving. *The true essence of common sense must become the core of our culture.*

During the 2016 Democratic primary elections, 13.2 million voters wanted paradigm-shift-magnitude change from the status quo to the concept of government of the people, by the people, and for the people. Those voters must be the agents of change who facilitate completion of the two prerequisites that will allow the new paradigms to be implemented.

Implementation of the new paradigms creates numerous pathways to re-making America. One such pathway, based on the development of alternate sources of funding, is presented in detail. The result is a government truly of the people, by the people, and for the people with the ability to pay off the federal debt and operate with a debt ceiling of zero while providing universal free health care, universal free education, a rigorous infrastructure program, benchmark social programs, and increased budgets for science and the environment.

WELCOME TO AMERICA

When striving to be the best, you must never underestimate the power of a negative. Remaking America must address the following negatives:

- Common sense is not common practice.
- We have a dysfunctional government.
- We have a mediocre education system.
- We have a dysfunctional election process.
- We have a dysfunctional foreign policy.
- We have a dysfunctional immigration policy.
- We have a dysfunctional criminal justice system.
- We have inadequate gun control.
- We have a dysfunctional taxation system.
- We have corruption and immorality everywhere.
- We value profit over people.
- We support abuses of power.
- We tolerate racism.
- Our infrastructure is crumbling.
- We have a military action culture.
- Our veterans are dying while waiting to see a doctor.
- We suppress innovation to benefit special-interest groups.
- We have disease care, not health care.

INTRODUCTION

As my engineering career evolved, I noticed that a lot of bad decisions were being made by highly educated people. The deeper I looked into the situation, it became apparent that the problem existed in all walks of life and at all levels of education. All of America agrees that "common sense is not common practice," but nothing is being done to change that! We cannot change because we do not understand what common sense is. Let's take a look at America's definition of common sense (Appendix A). What impression are you left with after you dig deeper into the meanings of the keywords? Correct. It is not a paradigm that reflects the character of a global leader! It has become a very weak and uninspiring collection of words. I decided to look for a definition that would capture the essence of common sense.

I found a powerful definition in the teachings of a twelfth century Japanese shogun, Yoritomo-Tashi. By the latter part of the twelfth century (i.e., 1186), greed, corruption, lawlessness, political intrigue, abuse of power, and total immorality had driven the Japanese empire into a state of demoralization. Sound familiar? The emperor selected Yoritomo-Tashi, one of the greatest statesmen that Japan has ever produced, to save the empire.

He defined common sense as the condition created by having certain positive mental characteristics (supports) overpowering negative mental characteristics (barriers) (Appendix B). Unfortunately ever since the birth of our nation, the barriers to common sense have evolved to become the core of our culture. This may be our last chance to prevent the total self-destruction of our culture and country. We must take the appropriate actions to base our new paradigm for common sense on the wisdom of Yoritomo-Tashi's common sense code of behavior.

Appendix C contains examples of no common sense that I have observed during my engineering career. A list of historical engineering disasters that have been analyzed in detail on the internet is presented if you crave more examples of no common sense. As you review the above examples, see if you can identify the supports of common sense that were missing and the barriers to common sense that dominated. At that point, you should appreciate the power of the new paradigm for common sense. You are on the way to developing the characteristics of a person having common sense.

- ▸ Focus the mind

- ▸ Grasp the situation

- ▸ Use of the power of approximation

Create your own list of situations from your life experiences that you feel reek of no common sense (i.e., personal relationships, politics, business, government, education, technology, health care, everyday life, etc.). What supports are missing? What barriers dominate?

Practice, practice, practice is the way to approach perfection!

LEARNING FROM THE PAST

- The constitution of the United States starts off, "We the people of the United States, *in order to form a more perfect union, establish justice, insure domestic tranquility, provide for the common defense, promote the general welfare, and secure the blessings of liberty to ourselves and our posterity,* do ordain and establish this constitution for the United States of America." It clearly defines the six critical objectives for the government.

- The founding fathers relied a great deal on the common sense of Thomas Paine to sort out the challenges of separating from the British Empire. Unfortunately that is where their use of common sense ended. Mr. Paine's use of common sense was a great help, but the essence of common sense was never adequately explained in his writings.

- President George Washington's warning about "the evils of political parties and entangling alliances abroad" was ignored right from the beginning.

- President George Washington once wrote: "A primary object should be the education of our youth in the science of government. In a republic, what species of knowledge can be equally important? And what duty is more pressing than communicating it to those who are the future guardians of the liberties of the country?"

- The president of the United States is elected by the Electoral College and not directly by the population! It only takes the votes of 270 of the Electoral College's 538 electors to elect the president. What an effective way to steal an election!

- In the late 1780s, the nascent United States of America was in trouble. In the words of the revered George Washington, "It was always moving upon crutches and tottering at every step," a crippled ship of state floundering at home and all but ignored abroad. "Without some alteration in our political creed," Washington warned, "the superstructure we have been…raising at the expense of so much blood and treasure must fall. We are fast verging to anarchy and confusion."

- In 1787 the founding fathers created the Constitution of the United States. Within that document was the framework for a government for "we the people" — and the framework for the Electoral College. The Electoral College was created because the founding fathers did not trust the judgment of the people when it comes to selecting a president and a vice president. That is why we have two elections to elect a president and a vice president.

General election — Millions of people vote to elect a president and vice president. It takes place on the Tuesday following the first Monday of November in years divisible by four. The candidates getting the most votes win.

Electoral College election — Electors, 538 representatives elected by the people, vote on the first Monday after the second Wednesday in December following the general election. The candidates getting 270 votes win. The Electoral College's results override the results of the general election!

There is no Constitutional provision or federal law requiring electors to vote in accordance with the popular vote in their states. Some states have such requirements. The Supreme Court has not specifically ruled on the question of whether pledges and penalties for failure to vote as pledged may be enforced under the Constitution. No elector has ever been prosecuted for failing to vote as pledged.

The United States Constitution contains very few provisions relating to the qualifications of electors.

Article II, section 1, clause 2 provides that no senator or representative, or person holding an office of trust or profit under the United States, shall be appointed an elector. As a historical matter, the Fourteenth Amendment provides that state officials who have engaged in insurrection or rebellion against the United States or given aid and comfort to its enemies are disqualified from serving as electors. This prohibition relates to post-Civil War.

There are no formal requirements for becoming an elector. Electors are often selected to recognize their service and dedication to their political party. They may be state elected officials, party leaders, or persons who have a personal or political affiliation with the presidential candidate. During the 2012 election cycle, an 18-year-old high school student was one of California's Electoral College electors. That action speaks for itself!

► Recording results of the popular votes did not start until 1824, a strange election. The winner received fewer electoral votes and fewer popular votes due to the presence of a three- man coalition as one of the candidates. From 1828 to 2016, forty-five elections took place. In four elections, the winner had fewer popular votes and more electoral votes than the other candidate (1876, 1888, 2000, and 2016).

The Electoral College is a tool that allows the political parties to override the popular vote.

► Right from the start, the United States Congress reneged on its pledge to:

▷ Form a more perfect union

▷ Establish justice

▷ Insure domestic tranquility

▷ Provide for the common defense

▷ Promote the general welfare

▷ Secure the blessings of liberty to ourselves and our posterity

The allegiance of political parties is to their political party, not the people! Primary objectives of the political parties are to:

▷ Raise money for the next election.

▷ Gain control of both houses (the Senate and the House of Representatives), and the office of the president. Maximize control!

▷ Keep the opposition party from making any progress. Manipulate legislation to favor the objectives of the party, various special interest groups, and wealthy donors to the party.

▷ Place judges on the bench of the Supreme Court that will favor the party's short- and long-term objectives.

▶ When a legislator pledges to vote for a piece of pending legislation, if the sponsor of that legislation inserts a specified amount of money to a particular organization or project in the legislator's home state or district, that is called earmarking (quid pro quo).

▶ Lobbying is a person acting for a special-interest group to influence the introduction or voting on legislation or the decisions of government administrators. *The Nation*, a weekly magazine of opinions and reviews, in 2014 suggested that while the number of 12,281 registered lobbyists was a decrease since 2002, lobbying activity was increasing and "going underground," as lobbyists use "increasingly sophisticated strategies" to obscure their activity. Analyst James A. Thurber estimated that the actual number of working lobbyists was close to 100,000 and that the industry brings in $9 billion annually.

- ▸ Gerrymandering is the redistricting of voting districts to the advantage of one party or disadvantage of a group, region, etc.

- ▸ Over the years, the greed, lawlessness, corruption, immorality, and political intrigue of the political parties created an attitude of indifference among "we the people." People stopped voting, took little interest in who the candidates were, what they stood for, and how the dynamics of government work. None of it mattered. Government was not working for "we the people." Votes from "we the people" filled the seats of Congress. "We the people" can also remove and replace the members of Congress. Votes are our only weapon against big money, special interests, and dysfunctional politics!

- ▸ Thomas Jefferson who believed laws and institutions must go hand in hand with the progress of the human mind, once wrote, "The tree of liberty must be refreshed from time to time with the blood of its patriots and tyrants. It is natural manure."

- ▸ President Dwight D. Eisenhower's warning about "the acquisition of unwarranted influence, whether sought or unsought by the Military-Industrial Complex. The potential for the disastrous rise of misplaced power exists and will persist" was also ignored.

- ▸ America has been at war 93 percent of the time — 225 out of 242 years —since 1776. The United States has never gone a decade without war. The only time the United States went five years without war (1935-1940) was during the isolationist period of the Great Depression.

- ▸ It is no surprise that war is good for those companies that provide the supplies needed for the war effort. World Wars I and II were milestones in the history of the United States.

World War I — Technology mechanized death! The use of airplanes, machine guns, and other advances in military weapons represented a paradigm shift in military operations.

World War II — Highlighted the need for optimum coordination between military and industrial operations, initiating the evolution of the Military-Industrial Complex (the United States military establishment and those industries producing military material, viewed as together exerting a powerful influence on foreign and economic policy).

Working under a cloak of secrecy, the Military-Industrial Complex forms alliances with select members of Congress and select special-interest groups to create and maintain a state of perpetual military preparedness for war and the development of war technologies. Most of their projects are top secret in order to protect national security. There is very little transparency regarding the nature and financing of projects. These alliances make the Military-Industrial Complex the most secretive and powerful organization in the United States and globally.

▶ America's nonstop, twenty-first century warfare has abused its servicemen and servicewomen via numerous tours of duty and failing to provide the timely health care and support they deserve.

▶ Regarding costs of major U.S. Wars (ref: Congressional Research Service: 7-5700, www.crs.govR522926): "Figures are problematic…because of difficulties in comparing prices from one vastly different era to another. Inflation is one issue, a dollar in the past would buy more than a dollar today. Perhaps a more significant problem is that wars appear vastly more expensive over time as the sophistication and cost of technology advances, both for military and civilian purposes. The estimates presented in this report, therefore, should be treated, not as truly comparable figures on a continuum, but as snapshots of vastly different periods of U.S. history." Nonetheless, a rough, low estimate of military costs of major U.S. wars from 1775-2010 comes to approximately $8 trillion (FY2011). A more current look at the cost of wars from 2001-mid-May 2016 comes to approximately $1.7 trillion (ref: The National Priorities Organization). One trillion dollars is a lot of money!

Let's see how far it goes. A U.S. $1 bill is approximately 2.5 inches wide by 6 inches long. One mile is equal to 5,280 feet. The distance from east coast to west coast for the U.S. is approximately 3,000 miles. Earth's diameter is approximately 7,926 miles. The moon is approximately 240,000 miles from Earth. One trillion $1 bills connected end to end will create a ribbon of money long enough to make approximately 31,600 trips across the U.S., 3,810 wraps around the Earth's equator, or 400 trips to the moon. Do the math!

▶ You do not have a process until it is definable, repeatable, and measurable. There are three performance levels for any process.

   ▷ Baseline — results obtained with the current equipment, materials, technology, and manpower.

   ▷ Entitlement — results obtained from optimization of current equipment, materials, technology, and manpower.

   ▷ Benchmark — results being obtained by the leader in the field, or outside of the field, via new paradigms for equipment, materials, technology, and manpower.

You must think "outside the box" to achieve benchmark performance. The best results often come from outside of your business and comfort zone.

▶ Never underestimate the power of a negative.

- A paradigm is a pattern, example, or model for success. When a paradigm shift takes place, everything goes back to zero. America needs to experience several paradigm shifts.

- It is human nature to repeat mistakes.

- The greatest barriers to innovation are vested interest and inertia.

- The root cause of any problem is one, or any combination, of three factors:

  ▷ Common sense is not common practice.

  ▷ Trying to be sophisticated before excelling at the basics.

  ▷ Not being a change agent.

- Academic Immigration? I received my bachelor of science degree in mechanical engineering in 1962. My first job was with one of the prime contractors for the Apollo space program. All engineers working on the project had to have a top-secret security clearance. During the vetting process, we were confined to a restricted area, not allowed to make contact with anyone working on the Apollo program, and denied access to any printed matter regarding the Apollo program. It usually took four to six weeks for the vetting process to be completed. In my case, it took longer because I had relatives living in Russia. National security was at risk because control of the moon was considered to be a major military advantage in the Cold War! In modern times, the national security is being challenged by terrorism.

- The mission-critical factor in developing a nation's economic strength is creating a superb education system that maximizes the development of each student's natural potential and minimizes the differences between the weakest and strongest students.

- When trying to be the best at anything, it is common sense to use the benchmark for that activity as your reference point for measuring or judging progress, quality, value, etc.

- Fear is the greatest motivator.

- If you focus on customer satisfaction and profit, everything else will fall into place.

- The guidelines for effective project planning and management are written in the sands of time with the blood of those who chose to ignore *them*.

    Good won't be fast.

    Good won't be cheap.

    Fast won't be cheap.

- What Should We Worry about at Night? The following remarks were made by retired Supreme Court Justice David Souter during a 2012 interview.

    "...I think some of the aspects of current American government that the people on both sides find frustrating are in part a function of the inability of people to understand how government can and should function. It is a product of civic ignorance. What I worry about is a remark that Benjamin Franklin made about how an ignorant people can never remain a free people. Democracy cannot survive too much ignorance....Franklin was asked by someone, I think on the streets of Philadelphia shortly after the 1787 Convention adjourned, what kind of government would the Constitution give us if it was adopted? Franklin's famous answer was, 'A republic if you can keep it. You cannot keep it in ignorance!'

    "I don't worry about our losing republican government in the United States because I'm afraid of a foreign invasion. I don't worry about it because I think there is going to be a coup by the military, as has happened in some other places.

"What I am worried about is that when problems are not addressed, people will not know who is responsible. And when the problems get bad enough as they might do — for example with another financial meltdown or serious terror attack — some one person will come forward and say, 'Give me total power, and I will solve this problem.' That is how the Roman republic fell. Augustus became emperor not because he arrested the Roman Senate. He became emperor because he promised that he would solve problems that were not being solved.

"If we know who is responsible, I have enough faith in the American people to demand performances from those responsible. If we don't know, we will stay away from the polls, we will not demand it, and the day will come when somebody will come forward, and we and the government will in effect say, take the ball and run with it. Do what you have to do. That is the way democracy dies. And if something is not done to improve the level of civic knowledge, that is what you should worry about at night."

UNDERSTANDING THE PRESENT

COMMON SENSE IS
NOT COMMON PRACTICE

A lack of common sense is the connecting thread in the patchwork quilt of America's negatives. It is the root cause of all the negatives. America has never understood the essence of common sense! (Ref: Introduction and Appendices A, B, and C). Acquiring that understanding is critical to the remaking of America. A new paradigm for common sense must become the core of America's culture!

Education

The most important resource that a nation has is its people. A superbly educated workforce is the key to developing a strong economy. The Department of Education is responsible for developing that resource. You would think that an activity of such importance to the future of a nation would warrant top-priority support. *Wrong*!

▸ The percentage of total spending allocated to a given activity, in a nation's budget, is a measure of how important the nation believes that activity is. In the 2015 budget for America, 2 percent was allocated to education, 1 percent to science, 1 percent to energy and environment, and 16 percent to the military.

▸ The relative decline of American education has long been a national embarrassment, as well as a threat to the nation's future.

- America spends more per pupil than any country in the world. Countries spend less on education and produce better students. In the recent past, funding for education in America has been reduced.

- America's students are not progressing to catch up to their peers in other industrialized countries.

- America's education system is not run by educators. American reform movements driven by millionaires and billionaires and free-market and privatization zealots with no real knowledge or understanding of public education continue to fall short of promised improvements (i.e., charter schools, cyber schools, vouchers, and corporate testing apparatus).

- Students are promoted through the system unprepared for success at each new level.

- Rigorous and comprehensive curriculum is sacrificed to prepare students for required standardized testing.

- As students leave high school unprepared for success at the college level, they have a hard time dealing with the college curriculum.

- Robust and comprehensive college curriculums are watered down to keep students in college. As a result of the curriculum adjustments, graduates are not prepared for success in the business world. Do you hear the dominos falling?

- Greedy bankers and politicians thwarted the free-education movement during the 1950s and 1960s to create the profit-generating education business we have today. Some students cannot afford to pay for college. Other students, and their families, go into debt to pay for a college education.

- Each year America's engineering talent pipeline loses experienced "old school" engineers by attrition (i.e., workforce reduction, restructuring, resignation, or retirement).

- Those engineers completed rigorous, comprehensive curriculums that provided the opportunity to develop the skills and knowledge that are prerequisites for success in the engineering workplace.

- The U.S. Commerce Department estimates that "by 2018 STEM employment will grow by 17 percent compared with 9 percent for other occupations." Unfortunately the U.S. will never be able to supply the engineering talent to fuel that growth from within its own borders unless some major paradigm shifts take place!

- Many college graduates entering the engineering talent pipeline are not adequately prepared to be effective in an engineering environment and leave the engineering career path after a short period of time.

- Legislators are considering increasing the number of visas to allow more foreigners to feed into the engineering talent pipeline. In general many of the foreign students return home a short time after graduation.

- The engineering component of K-12 STEM programs is not building strength due to a lack of teachers who can teach engineering. The ultimate result will be STeM (i.e., high school students not adequately prepared to be effective in an engineering environment), not STEM. Believe it or not, some mainstream college educators are considering certifying science teachers to teach engineering in K-STEM programs, the ultimate outcome being engineering as a subset of science (i.e., STeM).

- Many of the engineers exiting the talent pipeline are interested in teaching but are deterred by the large difference between engineering and teaching salaries.

- Many states have alternate-route programs to facilitate non-teachers becoming certified to teach specific subject areas, but they do not address the salary gap.

- The interaction between student and teacher is where knowledge is developed. That knowledge has a major impact on any country's economic strength. That is why that interaction must be optimized, not diminished! If it is not optimized, America's education system will never be more than mediocre.

- The government and the general public do not realize the impact that education has on a nation's economic strength. The general public considers education to be a secondary career with a ten-month year and minor stress.

- Working with our country's most valuable resource, to develop the knowledge that has a major impact on our economic strength and future development, should earn teaching the title of Most Valuable Career (MVC), deserving of the greatest respect and earning power of all other careers. Without teaching there would be no other careers!

- The current paradigm for America's education system is not structured to allow teaching to become the MVC.

- Increasing pressure to integrate technology into the teaching process may reduce the future role of teachers to that of an occasional proctor in the presence of students sent to a physical learning center (i.e., a computer lab).

- America's education system needs a major paradigm shift, and it needs it now!

Health Care

▶ Universal health care, sometimes referred to as universal health coverage, universal coverage, or universal care, usually refers to a health-care system that provides health care and financial protection to *more than 90 percent of the citizens* of a particular country. Since the definition of universal is *not limited or restricted*, the statement above is incorrect! The statement should read *almost universal health care, etc.*

▶ Usually free health care refers to a publicly funded health-care system that provides primary services free of charge *or for a nominal fee* to all its citizens, with no exclusions based on income or wealth. Since the definition for free is *no cost or payment*, the above statement is incorrect! The statement should read *almost free health care, etc.*

▶ *https://www.forbes.com/sites/merrillmatthews/2012/05/31/medicare-and-medicaid-fraud-is-costing-taxpayers-billions/#29b4c1d57331*

Barely a day goes by without a major news story highlighting some new Medicare or Medicaid scam that has bilked the government — that is, taxpayers — out of millions of dollars. Though most of the reports involve only a few people and scamming under $10 million, that's chump change compared to some of the bigger busts.

For example, federal authorities announced on May 2, 2012, they had arrested 107 health-care providers, including doctors and nurses, in several cities and charged them with cheating Medicare out of $452 million. To put this in perspective, the collapse of the solar company Solyndra, which had taken $535 million in taxpayer dollars from the Obama administration, has been a recurring topic in the media and public debates. The Medicare fraud arrest mentioned above was a news story for only a day or two. Or there was the 2010 story in which federal officials charged 94 people with $251 million in phony claims.

The problem is not new. Federal officials set up the Medicare Strike Force in 2007, which visited at random nearly 1,600 businesses in Miami, ground zero for Medicare fraud, that had billed Medicare for durable medical equipment. Officials found that nearly a third of the businesses, 481, didn't even exist, yet they had billed Medicare for $237 million over the previous year, according to National Public Radio. Indeed, scamming Medicare and Medicaid is so lucrative that the Russian and Nigerian mobs have gotten involved. And one of the New York crime families has moved to Florida because defrauding Medicare is both more lucrative and less dangerous than some of the traditional organized-crime activities.

And Medicaid is just as bad or worse. New York City has been a huge problem for Medicaid, with one former official suggesting that 40 percent of NYC's Medicaid payments are "questionable." *The New York Times*, in a multistory expose, reported that a Brooklyn dentist had filed 991 claims in one day. And while every state struggles with Medicaid fraud, the Office of Inspector General says the five topping the list are California, Texas, New York, Ohio, and Kentucky. The good news is that states recovered $1.7 billion in fraudulent payments in 2011. The bad news is the government had to spend $208 million to do it (*https://en.wikipedia.org/wiki/Medicare_fraud*).

Medicare fraud is typically seen in the following ways:

1. Phantom billing: The medical provider bills Medicare for unnecessary procedures or procedures that are never performed; for unnecessary medical tests or tests never performed; for unnecessary equipment; or equipment that is billed as new but is, in fact, used.

2. Patient billing: A patient who is in on the scam provides his or her Medicare number in exchange for kickbacks. The provider bills Medicare for any reason, and the patient is told to admit that he or she indeed received the medical treatment.

3. Upcoding scheme and unbundling: Inflating bills by using a billing code that indicates the patient needs expensive procedures.

We have disease care, not health care! The pharmaceutical industry is happy to keep patients alive with very expensive medications that have more dangerous side effects than positive medical outcomes. The focus of the medical community is on maintenance, not prevention, nutrition, or alternate techniques.

The cost of health care insurance gets more expensive each year. Many people cannot afford health care insurance and often must choose between food and medications.

Our veterans are dying while waiting for a visit with a doctor.

Government

The battlefield for remaking America is Congress! Our votes are the only weapon "we the people" have to fight the lobbyists, special-interest groups, large donors, and tainted politicians that cater to their needs. Our votes put them in Congress; our votes can remove and replace them!

▸ The federal government consists of three branches: legislative, judiciary, and executive.

▸ The legislative branch, aka Congress, makes all the laws, the judiciary branch makes sure the laws are followed, and the executive branch makes sure that everything else goes as planned.

▸ Congress consists of the Senate and the House of Representatives.

Congressional elections are held every two years on the Tuesday following the first Monday of November. The elections are always held in even numbered years. In a presidential election year, the president, all members of the House, and a third of the Senate face election.

Two years later the midterm elections occur. All House members are again up for election, along with another third of the Senate. Two years after that another presidential election is held, and the final third of the Senate is up for election, along with all House members.

- Members of the House of Representatives serve two-year terms while senators serve six-year terms.

- The votes of "we the people" determine who sits in what seats!

- At the start of each new Congress, the entire House of Representatives and one-third of the Senate are sworn into office. "I do solemnly swear (or affirm) that I will support and defend the Constitution of the United States against all enemies, foreign and domestic, that I will bear true faith and allegiance to the same; that I take this obligation freely, without any mental reservation or purpose of evasion; and that I will well and faithfully discharge the duties of the office on which I am about to enter. So help me God."

- The president takes an oath of office on inauguration day. "I do solemnly swear (or affirm) that I will faithfully execute the office President of the United States, and will to the best of my ability, preserve, protect and defend the Constitution of the United States."

- The preamble of the Constitution clearly presents the to-do list for the members of Congress and the president.

  ▷ Form a more perfect union

  ▷ Establish justice

  ▷ Insure domestic tranquility

  ▷ Provide for the common defense

  ▷ Promote the general welfare

  ▷ Secure the blessings of liberty to ourselves and our posterity

- While some individuals enter the field of politics with good intentions, the indifferent attitude of "we the people" toward politics (developed over decades) has made it possible for candidates of questionable integrity to become members of Congress. Too many people cannot name their senators or representatives in the house, let alone know what they stand for, their morality, how they vote, or their ability to represent us in Congress.

▸ America is in an advanced state of civic ignorance!

▸ Congress divides its legislative, oversight, and internal administrative tasks among approximately two hundred committees and subcommittees. In practice Congress functions not as a unified institution but as a collection of semiautonomous committees that seldom act in unison. Committee autonomy is a factor interfering with the adoption of a coherent legislative program.

▸ Congress does not have the ability to efficiently support approximately two hundred committees and subcommittees. The availability of the 535 members of Congress to work on the legislative process is reduced to approximately 107 net members (i.e., 50 percent of time raising money for the next election cycle and 40 percent typical workplace efficiency of white-collar office workers). The size of committees is too large (i.e., 26-61), and many members serve on multiple committees. A suitable analogy would be trying to put ten pounds of rice into a two-pound bag.

▸ America is committing fiscal suicide: uncontrolled spending without funding.

Politics

Decades of constant fighting to gain control of the government (i.e., the political parties), relentless attempts to manipulate the legislative process (i.e., special-interest groups and lobbyists), and the development of an attitude of indifference toward the democratic process (i.e., "we the people") have made

America a crippled republic, a breeding ground for the barriers to common sense, and a killing field for the supports for common sense!

- If the 2016 election cycle did not convince you that our political system is in dire need of a major paradigm shift, nothing will.

- The Democratic Party had two candidates. One represented continued improvements to the policies developed during the past eight years; the other wanted major paradigm shifts to make life better for the middle class and elimination of the influence that special-interest groups have on the political process. His own party did not want the magnitude of change that he stood for (i.e., "a political revolution") and used various elements of political intrigue to keep him from winning the primary election.

- The Republican Party had several candidates. One represented major changes to the status quo to "make America great again"; the others were just hungry to gain control of the country. The "make America great again" candidate tapped into the indifferent attitude of the voters toward the current political system with a hostile approach and became the forty-fifth president of America!

- The most unqualified candidate in American history was elected president.

- He did not win the general election.

- He won enough electoral votes to become president.

- Forty-seven percent of registered voters did not vote.

- He has no knowledge or understanding of how government can, or should, work.

- He has no experience as an elected public official at any level.

- He publicly demonstrated racist attitudes.

- He publicly demonstrated a lack of personal and business morals and ethics.

- He publicly demonstrated disrespect for women and minorities.

- He is a habitual liar.

- He promised to solve the problems that were not being solved, by himself if necessary.

- His lack of class, morals, ethics, and integrity was continually demonstrated during the entire election cycle.

- The Republican Party tried everything to discredit its own candidate but failed.

- He has no common sense! His character is defined by the barriers to common sense.

  ▷ *Sentimentality* — keeps him from putting his international financial empire into a blind trust. He prefers to have his sons manage the empire, which will result in serious concerns regarding future conflicts of interest in the president's decision-making process.

  ▷ *Egotism* — He thinks he is invincible. He believes that he can solve America's problems by himself if he has to. He is not a team player.

  ▷ *Moral Inertia* — He is incapable of change regarding the principles of right and wrong behavior.

  ▷ *Indifference* — He is indifferent regarding the national and global protocols for governance.

  ▷ *Illusion* — He thinks that America is just another company to be managed.

  ▷ *Impulse* — He does not think before speaking or acting. He has no foresight or self-control.

- When we cast our votes for the president, we are not voting for the president. We are voting for the Electoral College electors. Political parties in each state choose slates of potential Electoral College electors sometime before the general election. On Election Day, the voters in each state select their state's Electoral College electors by casting their votes for president. It only takes 270 Electoral College votes out of the 538 Electoral College electors to elect our president; yours is not one of them!

- Do you know who the Electoral College electors for your state are? What wisdom, knowledge, and experience do they have that qualifies them to select our president?

- Too many people do not monitor the voting record of their senators or members of the House of Representatives to check if they are looking out for the wants and needs of "we the people."

- Our indifferent attitude toward the democratic process must be replaced by a watchdog focus on Congress's performance! How did they vote? Why? What will it cost? How will it be funded?

- Let's take a look at how Congress is doing with what they pledged to do in the Constitution. Remember, it was the votes of "we the people" that filled the seats of Congress. We can remove and replace them with our votes!

Congress's Report Card

Form a More Perfect Union: F

The political parties think that a more perfect union is one in which one party controls the Senate, the House of Representatives, and the Oval Office. The allegiance of political parties is to the party, not the country or the people. They continue to make it harder for the people to vote and spend more time raising money for the next election then they do on legislative work. The special-interest groups are only too happy to help with the fundraising in return for future legislative considerations (i.e., quid pro quo).

Thanks to the indifferent attitude "we the people" have developed toward the democratic process, the low approval rating for members of Congress is rewarded with high reelection rates. Right from the beginning, the founding fathers "could not put the future of the country in the hands of ignorant farmers" (i.e., the Electoral College was created). Are we moving toward a more perfect union? I do not think so! We are going in the opposite direction!

Establish Justice: F

Justice is the use of authority and power to uphold what is right, just, or lawful. The personification of this, usually a blindfolded goddess holding scales and a sword, is that the laws and punishment for breaking the laws are the same for everyone.

- ▶ Is it just that "we the people" want stricter gun control laws but special-interest groups manipulate the legislative process to prevent that from happening (i.e., donations, gifts, and political-personal-business pressure).

- ▶ Is it just that veterans are dying while waiting for an appointment with a doctor?

- ▶ Is it just that we have disease care instead of health care? Special-interest groups focus on maintenance via pills and suppress prevention and natural remedies. Advertising for prescription drugs warns how the drug may harm or kill you! If you are taking multiple medications, the interaction between those medications is not fully understood.

- ▶ Is it just that only two diseases have been eradicated to date (i.e., polio and smallpox)?

- Is it just that big money buys you a better defense in a court of law?

- Is it just that large corporations pay no taxes while middle- and lower-income citizens struggle with taxes?

- Is it just that we have more people in prison than any other country on earth?

- Is it just that private corporations use lobbying expenditures and political contributions in an attempt to prevent legislation that would lower the number of people being put into prison?

- Is it just that under the federal Controlled Substance Act marijuana is a Schedule 1 drug, the same as heroin?

- Is it just that for-profit schools spend more money on marketing and recruiting than on actual instruction?

Insure Domestic Tranquility: F

Tranquility is the state of being calm, serene, free from disturbance or agitation, peaceful, placid, etc. Here are some reasons why domestic tranquility does not exist in America.

- In the richest country in the world, there are homeless people living in the streets. There are homeless families with children living out of their cars.

- Parents drop their children off to school and wonder if there will be a shooting episode that will kill their child.

- The cost of education is so high that some families cannot consider a college education for their children. Some parents may have to take out second and third mortgages on their home to pay for their child's education or the students borrow money and end up with tremendous debt after the education cycle.

- ▶ The current quality of education is mediocre at best. America is not keeping up with other industrial countries.

- ▶ It is hard to support a home, give children a decent education, take care of elderly parents, and save for a comfortable retirement.

- ▶ Taking care of elderly parents is a tremendous source of mental and financial stress.

- ▶ Childcare is a major stressor when it takes two full-time salaries to support a home.

- ▶ When is the next terrorist attack going to happen? Where? How?

- ▶ Congress is controlled by special-interest groups and big money. The needs and wants of "we the people" are not being addressed.

- ▶ America values power and money, not people.

- ▶ Global instability is a source of concern.

- ▶ The gap between those who have and those that do not have is growing!

- ▶ Race crimes are increasing.

- ▶ It is no longer safe to walk the streets alone, use the public parks, or enjoy local neighborhoods without the risk of being raped, mugged, or being an innocent victim of a shooting incident.

- ▶ Police-public relationships are disintegrating (i.e., use of excessive force, shooting unarmed suspects in the back during routine civil encounters).

Providing for the common defense has become a four-dimensional issue (i.e., defending borders, defending against terrorism beyond and within our borders, defending against cyberattacks, and defending democracy). Our ability to provide is eroding.

- America has been at war 93 percent of the time (225 out of 242 years) from 1776 to 2018.

- After World War II, America developed the most powerful military capabilities in the world.

- After World War II, the Military-Industrial Complex evolved into the most secretive and powerful organization in the world, with a mission to create and maintain a state of perpetual military preparedness for war and the development of war technologies. The defense of America's borders was well-established. The perceived enemy was the classical makeup of "boots on the ground" troops (i.e., troops between the ages of sixteen to forty fighting in large groups supported by air and sea capabilities).

- As America's foreign entanglements moved into different areas of the globe, the nature of the enemy changed (i.e., men, women, children, mothers, fathers, and grandparents, acting as individuals or in small groups, all willing to die for their country). Terrorism became the primary method of operation in their parent countries and within the borders of America! The common defense became more complicated.

- America's nonstop twenty-first century warfare has abused its servicewomen and servicemen via numerous tours of duty and failing to provide the health care and support they deserve.

- We are now faced with cyberattacks by foreign countries to interfere with our democratic processes.

- Internal issues are challenging America's democratic culture (i.e., immigration policies, dysfunctional government, hate crimes, wage inequality, health care, voting procedures and "we the people's" indifferent attitude toward the democratic process).

Promote the General Welfare: F

Here are some reasons why Congress is not promoting the general welfare.

- America is the only industrial nation in the world that does not provide almost free, almost universal, health care.

- America spends more on education than any other country in the world but does not produce the best students.

- Social Security, Medicare, and Medicaid provide a safety net for senior citizens. Instead of optimizing these systems (i.e., eliminating the abuse, fraud, price gouging and corruption of doctors, hospitals, contractors, insurance companies, and administrators), Congress uses the systems as a political football during the legislative process. They want to cut benefits to fund other programs that pander to special-interest groups.

- All Americans have a right to free education, free universal health care, and a stress-free retirement.

- Decades of the misuse of maintenance funding has resulted in a crumbling infrastructure.

- Special-interest groups and big money resist change and suppress new technologies to suit their means (i.e., global warming, renewable energy, natural cures, and nutrition).

- America's drug problems go unchecked.

- America's gun control issues go unchecked.

- America's immigration issues go unchecked.

- America's treatment of veterans is a disgrace.

- America is addicted to cellphone technology. Abuse of that technology is killing people on our roads and affecting the social skills of everyone in a negative way.

- The high cost of medications is forcing some senior citizens to decide between buying food or medicine.

Secure the Blessings of Liberty for Ourselves and Our Posterity: F

President George Washington had it right when he wrote, "a primary objective should be the education of our youth in the science of government. In a republic, what species of knowledge can be equally important? And what duty is more pressing than communicating it to those who are the future guardians of the liberties of the country." Apparently no one paid attention.

- All Congress has achieved since the writing of the Constitution is a crippled republic with a severe case of civic ignorance — just what the dark side of Congress wants!

- The dark side of Congress realizes that the public vote is what fills the seats of Congress. If the people do not know how government works, it is easier for the dark side to manipulate the legislative process to suit its political agenda.

- The limited civic education of America's youth and adults has been a concern for decades.

- Too many people cannot name the three branches of the federal government.

- Too many people cannot name the senators for their own state.

- Too many people cannot name their representatives in the House of Representatives.

- Too many people cannot name a single Supreme Court judge.

- Too many people do not know the beliefs, values, or morals of who they vote into Congress.

- Too many people do not monitor how their representatives vote on key issues.

- Too many people do not know the difference between a bill and a law.

- Too many people are ignorant of the congressional dynamics.

- The future of democracy depends on citizens who are motivated and able to participate effectively in the democratic process.

- The study of a comprehensive and rigorous civics curriculum should be a requirement for high school graduation and any program that grants citizenship to immigrants.

- Securing the blessings of liberty to ourselves and our posterity depends on our ability to change our indifferent attitude toward the democratic process to a proactive attitude toward keeping democracy alive.

DESIGNING THE FUTURE

Designing America's future will be a megaproject. The science of project management defines a process that consists of six major steps.

1. Project Statement — the project objective.

2. State the As-Is — a description of the present situation.

3. State the To-Be — a description of the ideal desired outcome.

4. Gap Analysis — identification of barriers that prevent the transition from As-Is to To-Be.

5. Create New Paradigms — to eliminate the Gap items.

6. Implementation — of new paradigms.

Now that the process has been defined, let's get started.

Project Statement

Design a set of paradigms that gives the people of America the ability to create a government of the people, by the people, and for the people!

As-Is

Decades of constant fighting to gain control of the government (i.e., the political parties), relentless attempts to manipulate the legislative process (i.e., special interest groups and lobbyists), and the development of an attitude of indifference toward the democratic process (i.e., we the people) have made

America a crippled republic, a breeding ground for the barriers to common sense, and a killing field for the supports of common sense!

To-Be

Representatives of the people, aka Congress, work together to achieve the goals presented in the Constitution.

- ▶ Form a more perfect union
- ▶ Establish Justice
- ▶ Insure domestic tranquility
- ▶ Provide for the common defense
- ▶ Promote the general welfare
- ▶ Secure the blessings of liberty to ourselves and our posterity

Gap Analysis

- ▶ National ignorance regarding common sense
- ▶ A mediocre education system
- ▶ A dysfunctional democratic process
  - ▷ People's indifference
  - ▷ The Electoral College
  - ▷ Political parties
  - ▷ Lobbying
  - ▷ Earmarks
  - ▷ Gerrymandering
  - ▷ Manipulation of the voting process

- ▷ Inadequate requirements for public service
- ▷ Abuses of power (i.e., Military-Industrial Complex, special-interest groups, and the super-rich)
- ▷ A dysfunctional immigration process
- ▷ A dysfunctional taxation system
- ▷ Flawed foreign policies
- ▷ A crumbling infrastructure
- ▷ A flawed set of values
    - ◇ Lack of gun control
    - ◇ Racism
    - ◇ Veterans' care
    - ◇ We have disease care, not health care
    - ◇ A military action culture
    - ◇ We value profit over people and quantity over quality
    - ◇ Corruption and immorality everywhere
    - ◇ Suppression of innovation to benefit special-interest groups
    - ◇ A dysfunctional criminal justice system

NEW PARADIGMS

PARADIGM — A PATTERN, EXAMPLE, OR MODEL FOR SUCCESS.

The following paradigms remove the barriers that prevent America from transitioning from its As-Is to the To-Be.

The chapter on implementation deals with how the barriers can be removed.

New Paradigms

Common Sense

MISSION — Change America's understanding of common sense from a meaningless collection of words to a powerful, personal strength for making decisions and solving problems.

BENCHMARK — The teachings of the twelfth century Japanese shogun, Yoritomo-Tashi (ref. Introduction and Appendices A, B, and C).

Developing an understanding of the essence of common sense, and its power to make decisions and solve problems, takes place on four levels of the education process.

- Early Child Development — from infant through two years.
- Primary and Secondary Education — Pre-K through Grade 2, Grades 3-5, Grades 6-12.
- Advanced Education — two-year and four-year colleges.
- Adult Education— adults needing a General Education Diploma (GED), immigrants applying for citizenship, lifelong continuing education.

Early Child Development

During this period, children mimic the sounds they hear and the behaviors they see. Parents and family must set a proper example by applying the principles of common sense to everyday life.

Primary and Secondary Education

Teaching begins at the very beginning of the formal teaching cycle.

- ▸ Pre-K through Grade 2. Discussions of simple, everyday situations of no common sense focus on identifying what caused the situation and how it could be fixed. The use of the terms barrier and support are introduced after the students have analyzed a number of situations and are comfortable with identifying causes and fixes. The first situations should focus on classroom activities, expand to situations at home, and finally include situations beyond the classroom and home. A frequency of two situations per week, allowing five to ten minutes per situation, is an arbitrary starting point which would vary depending on class capabilities.

- ▸ From Grades 3-5, an understanding of the relationships between barriers and supports is developed. Situations analyzed include historical events. A frequency of three situations per week, allowing ten to fifteen minutes per situation, is an arbitrary starting point which would vary depending on class capabilities.

- ▸ From Grades 6-12, an understanding of how to develop supports, avoid barriers, and use common sense to make decisions and solve problems is developed. Situations analyzed include futuristic events. A frequency of four to five situations per week, allowing fifteen to twenty minutes per situation, is an arbitrary starting point which would vary depending on class capabilities.

- ▸ Demonstrating a thorough understanding of the essence of common sense and the ability to use common sense to make decisions and solve problems is a requirement for high school graduation.

Advanced Education

During a four-year college experience, the outline for a course on common sense will be constant.

- ▶ Review basic principles.

- ▶ Understand the relationship between barriers and supports.

- ▶ Analysis of situations that are examples of no common sense.

- ▶ How to develop the three characteristics of a person with common sense.

    - ▷ Focus the mind

    - ▷ Grasp the situation

    - ▷ Use the power of approximation

- ▶ Common sense and problem solving — the root cause of any problem is one, or any combination, of three factors.

    - ▷ Common sense is not common practice.

    - ▷ Trying to be sophisticated before excelling at the basics.

    - ▷ Not being a change agent.

The course will run for the entire year, meeting three times a week for ninety minutes.

Demonstrating a thorough understanding of the essence of common sense, and the ability to use common sense to make decisions and solve problems, is a requirement for graduation.

Adult Education

The common sense course outline utilized for the Advanced Education program will be an integral part of the GED, citizenship, and general adult education programs. The course will run for twenty weeks, meeting once a week for a two-hour session. The program will be held in appropriate public facilities.

Demonstrating a thorough understanding of the essence of common sense, and the ability to make decisions and solve problems, is a requirement for meaningful completion of the program.

New Paradigms

Education 2.0

MISSION — maximize the development of each student's inherent potential and minimize the difference between the best student and the worst student.

BENCHMARK — Finland's education system has evolved into a benchmark for all nations (ref. Appendix D).

- All public education is free from daycare through adult education. Funding and management of the system is provided by the federal government. The system consists of:

  - Daycare — Infants and Toddlers, assess development potential.

  - Preschool — Five-year-olds, emphasis on play and socializing.

  - Pre-K — Six-year-olds, emphasis on play and socializing. Begin some academics.

  - Elementary School — Ages 7-12, Grades K-5, develop knowledge and socialization skills.

  - Middle School — Ages 13-15, Grades 6-8, develop knowledge and socialization skills.

  - High School — Ages 16-19, Grades 9-12, develop knowledge and socialization skills.

  - College — Develop knowledge, bachelor's degree.

- ▷ Postgraduate — Expand knowledge, master's degree, doctor's degree.

- ▷ Professional Development — Certification of specific skills.

- ▷ Adult Education — Personal development, General Education Diploma (GED), obtain citizenship, subjects to improve quality of life.

- ► The system is managed by educators, not business people, military leaders, or career politicians.

- ► Schools provide food, medical care, counseling, and transportation if needed.

- ► There is a national curriculum. A superbly educated workforce has a major impact on the development of a country's economy. Private schools must teach the national curriculum.

- ► Every school, public and private, has the same national goals and draws from the same pool of university-trained educators.

- ► All curricula are comprehensive and rigorous.

- ► There are no classes for gifted students.

- ► The focus is on the student/teacher interface, where knowledge is developed.

- ► The maximum class size is ten students.

- ► There is no standardized testing.

- ► Diagnostic testing of students is used early and frequently. If a student is in need of extra help, intensive intervention is provided.

- ► There is no homework.

- ► Grades are not given until high school, and even then class rankings are not compiled.

- Students are separated into academic and vocational tracks after the first two years of high school.

- Groups of teachers visit each other's classes to observe their colleagues at work. Teachers also get one afternoon per week for professional development.

- Three new curricula are added to the traditional curricula: Common Sense, Education 2.0, and the Dynamics of Democracy. Demonstrating a thorough understanding of the essence of Common Sense and The Dynamics of Democracy is a requirement for high school graduation.

- Understanding The Dynamics of Democracy prepares students for a proactive role in the democratic process or a career in politics.

- Teaching is the most respected and most difficult degree to obtain.

- A master's degree in teaching is required to become a teacher in the system. Only the top 10 percent of the graduating class will be considered.

- Teaching is a high-status profession.

- Teachers mold America's most valuable resource, its people, into a world-class educated workforce.

- Teaching careers have the highest salary levels of all careers. Without teachers there would be no other careers.

New Paradigms

Dynamics of Democracy

MISSION — To remake America's crippled republic.

BENCHMARK — Common sense.

- There are no political parties, just guardians of the Constitution and the democratic process.

- There is no Electoral College.

- Since there are no political parties, there is no need for a Democratic National Committee (DNC) or a Republican National Committee (RNC).

- Congress still consists of the Senate and the House of Representatives.

- Since there are no political parties, the number of senators is reduced to fifty.

- All planning and attempts to manipulate the legislative process to benefit any individual, special-interest groups, or publicly elected officials are a federal crime, punishable by extreme fines and lifetime banishment from public service. Any person having knowledge of such planning or actions against America who does not report it to the Federal Bureau of Investigation is just as guilty as the perpetrators.

- The following actions are federal crimes.

> ▷ Lying to Congress

> ▷ Lobbying

> ▷ Gerrymandering

> ▷ Earmarking (pro-quid-pro arrangements between members of Congress)

- ► Members of Congress no longer have to raise funds for election campaigns. The new paradigm for the election process eliminates the need for campaign donations.

- ► Legislative Teams, formerly known as subcommittees, must have three, five, or seven permanent voting members. Temporary ad hoc members may be added in special cases only. Each member of Congress may be a permanent member of only one Legislative Team at a time. They may be ad hoc members of no more than two Legislative Teams at a time.

- ► All roll-call votes must record the vote, the subject of the vote, the reason for voting that way, and how the issue will be funded. All results will be posted on the internet for public review within forty-eight hours of the vote.

- ► Passage of a bill in the House of Representatives requires 75 percent of the votes.

- ► Passage of a bill in the Senate requires 75 percent of the votes.

- ► The president signs a bill into law.

- ► Congress can override a presidential veto with 90 percent of the vote.

- ► Each member of Congress must post a quarterly list of accomplishments on the internet for review by the public.

- ► Each member of Congress must post a quarterly list of the votes missed and the reason for missing the votes on the internet for review by the public.

New Paradigms

The Election Process

MISSION — Create a voting process that is as simple as possible for all citizens of America and prevents cybermanipulation.

BENCHMARK — Common sense.

- Citizens take a proactive role in the democratic process. We vote! We constantly monitor the performance of the elected officials to make sure they focus on the important to-do list stated in the Constitution (i.e., quarterly progress reports on the internet). When they go off point, we replace them! We get to know the candidates for public office. What are their beliefs, morals, and values? Do they understand how the democratic process works? Why do they want to represent the people? How are they viewed by their peers? Are they qualified to do the job?

- There is no Electoral College. When we vote for the president, we vote for the president, not an electoral voter!

- There is no need for campaign donations. They are illegal.

- Each level of government (i.e., municipal, county, state, and federal) will create an appropriate Board of Elections that will manage the election process.

Post Openings — descriptions and requirements for positions to be voted on during the next election will be distributed to all post offices and libraries.

Letters of Interest — persons interested in running for office may submit letters of interest, in person, that indicate how they meet the job requirements and what they believe are the three top challenges of the job. Each letter of interest will be limited to one standard 8½" x 11" page, single spaced with a 14-point font. Letters of Interest will be accepted for a period of two weeks at post offices and libraries and must contain the name and Social Security Number of the interested person. When the letter is submitted, the person will be fingerprinted.

The Board of Elections will collect all the letters of interest from the post offices and libraries, combine them to form a composite package of the letters of interest, and deliver copies of the composite package to all post offices and libraries.

Public Review — Potential voters will obtain the composite package of the Letters of Interest from their local post office or library. Public review of the composite package will take place during a specified three-week period. During that period, each potential voter will select three potential candidates from the composite package. The selections must be submitted on one standard 8½" x 11" page, single spaced, with a 20-point font. The potential voter's review must contain their name and Social Security Number. The format for the review will be...

- ▶ Potential voter's name
- ▶ Potential voter's Social Security Number
- ▶ Candidate #1 — Excellent
- ▶ Candidate #2 — Very Good
- ▶ Candidate #3 — Good
- ▶ The completed review is submitted to the appropriate post office or library, and the potential voter will be fingerprinted.

Selection of Candidates — All public reviews will be collected from the post offices and libraries by the Board of Elections and analyzed to select three candidates for the ballot. A score for each of the potential candidates identified in the public reviews will be calculated using the following technique.

Total Score = A + B + C
A = (the number of Excellent votes)(3)
B = (the number of Very Good votes)(2)
C = (the number of Good votes)(1)

The three candidates with the highest total score will be put on the ballot. In case of a tie, the candidate with the most excellent votes breaks the tie.

Campaigning — Will take place during a one-month period prior to the election period. There will be no debates. Each candidate will get a fifteen-minute television segment to state his or her case. The appropriate level of government will pay for the television time. During the month prior to the election period, the candidates may give as many interviews with the press and public radio and conduct as many town hall meetings as time allows.

Voting — Will take place over nine consecutive days (i.e., one two-day weekend + five work days + one two-day weekend, sixteen hours per day (6 A.M. - 10 P.M.) at conveniently located voting places.

Registered voters will sign in at Board of Election tables, where they will be given a ballot sheet (sample ballot sheets will have been mailed to registered voters as soon as the ballot sheet was formalized.). Voters will proceed to a voting booth, where they will find a table and a chair. Using a pen or pencil provided, their votes are cast by manually placing checks next to the candidates of choice. After casting their votes, they will exit the voting booth and proceed to the next station: a table and two chairs, where a voting monitor (a volunteer approved by the Board of Elections) confirms that the ballot sheet has been properly completed. If there are no issues, the voter signs and dates the ballot sheet, and the voting monitor places it into an appropriate lockbox. If there are issues, the voter is directed to another station, where a voting monitor will resolve the issues. Once all issues are resolved, the voter signs and dates the ballot sheet, and the voting monitor places it into the appropriate lockbox. At the end of the voting day, all lockboxes are transported to the Board of Elections headquarters by a member of the National Guard, or an appropriate law officer, and the counting of that day's votes begins. Homebound voters may request a ballot sheet from the Board of Elections and mail in their vote during the nine-day voting period.

Vote Counting — Done by election monitors, and results for each voting day are reported to the Board of Elections. All results are kept secret until the results of the nine voting days are compiled into a final result. The head of the Board of Elections reports the final results to the appropriate level of government (i.e., mayor, governor, and attorney general) for release to the public and the media.

New Paradigms

Health Care

MISSION — Create a free, inclusive, single-payer health care system for all of America's citizens.

BENCHMARK — There is no benchmark for a free, inclusive, single-payer health care system. When implemented, America's health care system will be the benchmark for the rest of the world.

- All citizens have free access to any needed services, including dental and vision.

- Doctors receive annual salaries plus bonuses based on improved outcomes. Salaries are based on the knowledge required and the risk to the patient's well-being (i.e., general practitioner, specialist, surgeon, etc.).

- The use of natural cures and nutrition are thoroughly investigated prior to the use of pharmaceuticals.

- Transportation to and from office visits, testing facilities, and hospital stays is provided when the use of private or public transportation is impractical.

- House calls are made when no other travel options are practical.

- Initial doctor/patient consultations may be conducted via advanced communication technology when possible.

- To eliminate mistakes caused by fatigue, all operatives of the system (i.e., nurses, nurse's aides, general practitioners, specialists, surgeons, etc.) will work together to determine common sense patient loads for a standard eight-hour shift.

- ▸ Any employee who knows about fraudulent billing is just as guilty as the people perpetrating the fraud and will be punished accordingly.

- ▸ Any employee who reports fraudulent billing will get 50 percent of the gross savings realized, tax free.

- ▸ Private hospitals and other medical facilities must comply with the national standards.

New Paradigms

Immigration

MISSION — Create a system that welcomes people from other countries who want to call America their home and to protect America from people who want to harm America.

BENCHMARK — A proven technique for protecting national security (ref. Learning from the Past, Academic Immigration).

- Each and every immigrant entering America, or illegally residing in America, must obtain a National Security Clearance (NSC) before they can participate in the democratic process. An NSC consists of extensive reviews of their medical condition and political leanings. Chain immigration is illegal.

- Immigration Transitioning Centers (ITC), located on each of America's borders, will house all people seeking permanent residence in America until extensive reviews of their medical condition and political leanings are determined. The location and number of ITC will be determined by the number of immigrants and their points of entry. The ITC will consist of an arrangement of self-sustaining modules (i.e., residence, services, administrative, etc.) that can be moved from one location to another. After completion of medical and political reviews and creation of the appropriate documentation, the immigrants may move to a preferred location in the United States and must enroll in a program to become an American citizen.

- Any person from another country wanting to work in America for an extended period of time must obtain an NSC before they may apply for a Green Card.

- Any person from another country wanting to vacation or do business in America for a short period of time must obtain an NSC before he or she may apply for a travel permit.

- Any American citizen wanting to vacation or do business for a short period of time in a foreign country must obtain a modified NSC (without having to be housed in an ITC) before he or she may apply for a travel permit.

- Travel permits may be issued for periods of thirty, sixty, or ninety days. Requests for a travel permit must be made thirty days before the start of the travel period. If a group is involved, each member of the group must have his or her own NSC and travel permit.

- Undocumented immigrants have ninety days to get documented or face deportation.

  ▷ Any individual who has lived and worked in America for at least five years, without a criminal record, and wants to live in America permanently must file appropriate documents and apply for citizenship.

  ▷ If the individual wants to stay, a penalty income tax of 1 percent will be paid for each year that the individual was undocumented.

  ▷ If a criminal record exists, the individual must submit to the appropriate authorities or be deported. Some criminal convictions lead to deportation. Some of the main ones are aggravated felonies, drug convictions, crimes of moral turpitude, firearms conviction, crimes of domestic violence, and other criminal activity. Immigration law has other grounds for deportation (for example, if you over-stayed your visa, committed marriage fraud, are a threat to the security of America, voted unlawfully, or falsely claimed to be an American citizen after September 30, 1996). After deportation a person must wait either five or ten years (depending on the case) before returning to America legally. After a second deportation, the wait is twenty years. If you are deported for an aggravated felony, you can probably never return to America.

- Minor children (less than eighteen years of age) who were not born in America must obtain the appropriate documentation and apply for citizenship when they reach the age of eighteen years. If both parents are deported for legal reasons, that minor child must leave with the parents. If the father is deported and the mother decides to stay, the minor child must stay with the mother. If the mother is deported and the father decides to stay, the minor child must go with the mother.

- Minor children born in America are automatically American cit-izens and should have the usual documentation (i.e., birth cer-tificate, Social Security Number, etc.). If the parents of an American citizen who is less than eighteen years old are de-ported, the minor child must go with the parents. If guardian-ship of the minor child is transferred to a family member who is an American citizen living in America, the minor child may stay with that family member.

- Passports — All existing and new applications for a United States passport must be evaluated via a modified NSC. If a United States passport has been inactive for three years, it must be reevaluated via a modified NSC.

- Foreign Passports — Must be evaluated via a modified NSC be-fore they can be used to enter the United States of America. If a foreign passport has been inactive for three years, it must be reevaluated via a modified NSC.

New Paradigms

Domestic Affairs

MISSION — Insure domestic tranquility and promote the general welfare.

BENCHMARK — Common sense

- Universal health care and education are free.

- All senior citizen services are free.

- The minimum wage is $15 per hour, and increases are tied to cost-of-living increases.

- Not paying men and women equal wages for equal work is illegal.

- The diversity of law enforcement units must reflect the diversity of the communities they work in.

- The law enforcement/community interface reflects a mutual concern for the protection and safety of the community, not a conflict between the community and an invading army!

- Recreational use of marijuana is legal.

- The privatization of prisons is illegal. All prison facilities are run by federal, state, or local employees.

- It is illegal for a private citizen to own a weapon of war (i.e., any semiautomatic or automatic weapon or device designed for military operations). Private citizens over twenty-one years of age must complete a comprehensive application process that justifies the possession and use of any firearm (i.e., collecting, hunting, competition shooting, and self-protection). Failure to complete such an application is a federal offense!

- Race crimes are a federal offense.

- There is no federal income tax.

- There is no FICA payroll deduction.

- All federal spending is paid for with alternate sources of funding (ref. page 69).

- The federal debt ceiling is zero!

New Paradigms

Foreign Affairs

MISSION — Change from a war culture to a proactive global leader.

BENCHMARK — Common sense

- America will participate in a global economy in a fair and just manner.

- America will respect any country's right to establish political and religious freedom.

- America will not try to convert any country's political system to a democratic system.

- America will report any unfair business practices and/or human-rights issues to the United Nations for review and determination of appropriate follow-up actions.

- As a member of the United Nations, America will be a proactive agent of change to define actions that will secure the health of Planet Earth for ourselves and our posterity.

- America will conduct an organized withdrawal from countries that were drawn into military actions without appropriate justification (i.e., Afghanistan, Pakistan, Iraq, and Syria).

- America will revisit post-World War II agreements that still require the presence of American "boots on the ground." Advancements in technology and changes in the nature of the enemy have made "boots on the ground" military power obsolete (i.e., drones, cyberattacks, nuclear weapons, robotics, stealth aircraft, missile defense systems, terrorist groups, lone wolf terrorists, homegrown terrorists).

- ▸ America must become the global leader in cybertechnology.
- ▸ America will focus its military priorities on defense of the United States and its holdings.

NEW PARADIGMS

REQUIREMENTS FOR PUBLIC SERVICE CAREERS

MISSION — Create a combination of academic and practical requirements that define the skills and knowledge that are prerequisites for success in a career in politics.

BENCHMARK — Common sense. There is no benchmark. When this paradigm is implemented, it will be the benchmark for all democratic countries.

- A political career can take place on one, or all, of four levels.

  ▷ Municipal — mayor and any other elected or appointed governing officials.

  ▷ County — freeholders and any other elected or appointed governing officials.

  ▷ State — governor and any other elected or appointed governing officials.

  ▷ Federal — president, vice president, senator, representative, and any other elected or appointed governing officials.

- A political career must begin at an academic level. The entrance requirements for a career in politics are bachelor's and master's degrees in the new government curriculum: Dynamics of Democracy (ref. New Paradigm, Education 2.0, pages 41-43).

- Requirements for the four levels of government:

  ▷ Municipal — Minimum age: Twenty-five years. Bachelor's and master's degrees in The Dynamics of Democracy.

  ▷ County — Minimum age: Thirty years. Bachelor's and master's degrees in The Dynamics of Democracy. Five years of experience at the municipal level.

  ▷ State — Minimum age: Thirty-five years. Bachelor's and master's degrees in The Dynamics of Democracy. Five years of experience at the county level, five years of experience at the municipal level.

  ▷ Federal — Minimum age: Forty-five years. Bachelor's and master's degrees in The Dynamics of Democracy. Ten years of experience at the state level, five years of experience at the county level, five years of experience at the municipal level.

  ▷ Requirements for the offices of president and vice president —Minimum age: Fifty-five years. Bachelor's and master's degrees in The Dynamics of Democracy. Five years of experience at the federal/domestic level, five years of experience at the federal/foreign level, ten years of experience at the state level, five years of experience at the county level, five years of experience at the municipal level.

New Paradigms

Term Limits

MISSION — Create a system of terms and term limits that is in sync with the dynamics of an evolving nation.

BENCHMARK — Thomas Jefferson, who believed laws and institutions must go hand in hand with the progress of the human mind, once wrote, "The tree of liberty must be refreshed from time to time with the blood of its patriots and tyrants. It is natural manure."

Position	Term Years	Term Limit
President	4	3
Vice President	4	3
Senator	4	2
Representative	2	4
Governor	4	2
Supreme Court Judge	5	2

New Paradigms

The Supreme Court of the United States

MISSION — Increase productivity and relevance to the diversity of America.

BENCHMARK — Thomas Jefferson, who believed laws and institutions must go hand in hand with the progress of the human mind, once wrote, "The tree of liberty must be refreshed from time to time with the blood of its patriots and tyrants. It is natural manure."

▸ There will be three federal supreme courts with seven full-time members and two ad hoc alternates. In case of a tie, an ad hoc alternate will be used to break the tie. The diversity of each court must be the same as that of America.

▸ The minimum age is sixty years, with thirty years of experience evenly spread across the spectrum of other federal courts.

▸ Each justice may serve two five-year terms and must retire at seventy years of age.

▸ A simplified version of the new election process is used to select new justices. Members of the judicial branch may declare themselves, or recommend another, as a candidate. A judicial branch selection committee narrows down the list of potential candidates to create a reasonable-sized ballot. Congress votes to select new justices from that ballot.

New Paradigms

Implementation

Remaking America depends on our ability to send representatives to Congress who will focus on the needs and wants of the American people. That is why having a common sense culture and a state of civic intelligence are prerequisites for success. We must pick our representatives carefully, know what their values are, what their morals are, and their motives for wanting to be our representatives. When they are in office, we must monitor their performances and act accordingly when they forget why they are there. We must vote at all appropriate elections and replace poor performers with more suitable candidates.

The 13.2 million voters in the 2016 Democratic presidential primary election who wanted to establish a government of the people, by the people, and for the people marked the start of the political revolution that is needed to save our republic! Those voters must become the agents of change who facilitate the creation of a common sense culture and a state of civic intelligence. They must fuel a grassroots, nationwide awareness program engaging family members, friends, neighbors, and business associates and focusing on one-on-one personal contact, community center seminars, and the use of social media, radio, television, and any other communication techniques that get out the message.

Once the common sense culture and the state of civic intelligence are realized, the paradigm shift legislative changes required to implement the new paradigms will be possible!

New Paradigms

Alternate Sources of Funding

The following alternate sources of funding have tapped into the immense wealth of our democratic system, addressed the poor efficiency of federal civilian workers, addressed the tremendous degree of fraud in key social programs, drawn from the most powerful special-interest groups in the world, and took advantage of some of our most dangerous social habits. They do not force any financial requirements upon the general public. The obligations presented below cannot be passed down to the general public!

Source	$
1% tax on currency traded	5,148,000,000,000
Reduction of Medicare fraud	196,000,000,000
1% tax on bank assets	131,382,400,000
Increased efficiency of federal workforce	58,300,000,000
1% tax on insurance co. assets	44,164,100,000
1% tax on imports	22,482,090,000
Quarterly national 50/50 raffles (tax-free)	17,500,000,000
1% tax on exports	14,504,570,000
1% tax on entertainment & media revenue	8,040,000,000
1% tax on gas & oil revenue	6,832,900,000
1% tax on Amazon U.S. revenue	3,652,000,000
1% tax on pharmaceutical revenue	3,373,000,000
1% tax on alcoholic beverage revenue	2,232,000,000
1% tax on airline revenue	1,582,000,000
1% tax on tobacco revenue	1,212,268,000

1% tax on Pentagon war spending	912,500,000
1% tax on casino gambling	731,000,000
1% tax on pro sports revenue	361,410,400
Tax on shares traded, (0.01)$/share	355,831,673
1% tax on local TV revenue	327,800,000
1% tax on amusement park revenue	146,000,000
1% Tax on gun & ammo revenue	135,000,000
1% tax on private prison revenue	36,800,000

TOTAL = $5,662,263,670,073

Three of the most important new paradigms for remaking America are universal free health care, universal free education, and a robust infrastructure program. Initial cost estimates for those activities are $1.4 trillion, $0.71 trillion and $1.0 trillion, respectively, for a total of $3.11 trillion per year.

Appendix E contains the appropriate references, assumptions, and calculations for the results presented above.

The analysis presented above indicates that *where there is a will, there is a way!* The financial institutions and business sectors referred to have built their empires on the back of America, caring only about the bottom line (i.e., hiding revenue offshore, manipulating the legislative process, and putting company and profit before country)! They are not the only ones (i.e., sales of automobile manufactures, assets of primary contractors for the Pentagon, etc.). It is time for big business and big money to become part of TEAM AMERICA!

Imagine what could be accomplished with a 2 percent or 3 percent model.

If reducing Medical fraud and increased efficiency of the federal workforce are considered one-time benefits...

A net 1% model results in $5,407,963,670,073 of funding.

A net 2% model results in $10,815,927,340,146 of funding.

A net 3% model results in $16,223,891,010,219 of funding.

CONCLUSION

America is a crippled republic! It is crippled because of two root causes.

1. America's ignorance regarding the true meaning of common sense.

2. America suffers from a severe condition of civic ignorance, resulting in an indifferent attitude toward the democratic process.

During the 2016 presidential primary elections, a grassroots movement to remake America was created (i.e., the Senator Sanders campaign). The momentum created by that grassroots movement must increase to eliminate the root causes presented above and to facilitate the successful implementation of new paradigms. If the root causes are not eliminated, the republic will die!

When Americans look "outside the box" and passionately participate in the democratic process, understand how government should work, and know the essence of common sense, tremendous things can be achieved. We can have universal free health care, universal free education, world-class infrastructure, and benchmark social programs. We can remake America and be a global benchmark!

Appendix A

America's Definition for Common Sense

- The *unreflective opinions* of *ordinary* people.

- Sound and prudent, but often *unsophisticated*, judgement.

UNREFLECTIVE — lack of thought and deliberation.

OPINION — belief stronger than an impression and less strong than positive knowledge. A generally held view.

ORDINARY — routine, usual, poor, inferior.

UNSOPHISTICATED — lacking complexity of structure, simple. Not worldly or wise.

APPENDIX B

A NEW PARADIGM
FOR COMMON SENSE

"The quality popularly designated as Common Sense comprehends, according to the modern point of view, the sound judgment of mankind when reflecting upon problems of truth and conduct without bias from logical subtleties or selfish interests....*It is one of Nature's priceless gifts, an income in itself. It is as valuable as its application is rare.*"

— Yoritomo-Tashi, circa 1186

To acquire common sense, one must develop the nine supports of common sense that will overcome the barriers to common sense.

SUPPORTS	BARRIERS
Perception	Moral inertia
Memory	Indifference
Thought	Sentimentality
Alertness (mental activity)	Egotism
Reason	Illusion
Deduction	Impulse
Foresight	
Judgment	
Self-Control	

Definitions

Supports

1. *Perception* — awareness of the elements of environment through physical sensation.

2. *Memory* — the capacity for, or act of, remembering.

3. *Thought* — the act or process of thinking.

4. *Alertness (mental activity)* — quick to perceive and act.

5. *Reason* — to take part in conversation, discussion, or argument.

6. *Deduction* — the deriving of a conclusion by reasoning.

7. *Foresight* — a view forward.

8. *Judgment* — the process of forming an opinion or evaluation by discerning and comparing.

9. *Self-Control* — restraint exercised over one's own impulses, emotions, or desires.

Barriers

1. *Moral inertia* — indisposition to change relating to principles of right and wrong in behavior.

2. *Indifference* — absence of a compulsion (a drive or urge) to or toward one thing or another.

3. Sentimentality — the quality or state of being sentimental, especially to excess or in affection.

4. *Egotism* — an exaggerated sense of self-importance.

5. *Illusion* — something that deceives or misleads intellectually.

6. *Impulse* — a sudden, spontaneous inclination or incitement to some unpremeditated act.

Appendix C

Examples of No Common Sense

A global medical device company was in the process of developing a colostomy collection pouch to expand its current product line. The design required the assembly of multiple layers of plastic films in a specific orientation to achieve the desired flow path into the collection area. The relative position of one layer of film to adjacent layers of film was critical to the performance of the collection pouch.

The process development team came up with a simple, inexpensive change to the usual process that would make it impossible to misassemble the critical film layers. The plant manager vetoed the idea, guaranteeing that 100 percent inspection by machine operators and quality-control technicians during production would produce the required assembly of the pouch.

The product delivered to the sales division the day before the national product launch had a leakage rate of 20 percent.

The five-year growth plan of a major pharmaceutical company created the need to fill several high-level executive positions. It was decided that the internal talent pool did not contain the experience required to function at the high-level executive positions created, and a recruiting program to bring in executives from outside of the company was initiated.

After five years, a review of the growth plan indicated that a majority of the executives hired from outside of the company resigned after three years.

They all had the same reason for leaving: The company had pressured them to change their management styles to fit the culture of the company. They weren't given the opportunity to "do their thing."

At the same time, it was noticed that a large number of the internal talent pool had left the company because there was no opportunity for advancement to higher executive positions. The company had lost a great deal of money on the outside executive hunt and weakened the internal talent pool.

A manufacturer of church pews was having trouble keeping up with the increase in sales. The plant was operating two full-time shifts and a partial third shift when sales peaked. The current process involved joining wooden parts using a cumbersome gluing technique: apply glue, assemble and clamp parts, allow glue to cure, and remove excess glue when needed. Soon a full third shift would be needed. It was time to develop a new manufacturing process/equipment to improve quality, reduce cycle time, and eliminate the need for multiple shifts and overtime.

An engineering consulting firm was selected and project requirements agreed upon. The project plan called for delivery of the first new machine in nine months. The engineering consulting firm would install the equipment, establish operating procedures, train operators, and oversee start-up. A start-up team of two engineers and two technicians delivered the equipment on time, and the equipment was meeting all the agreed upon requirements within one week.

Three days after the start-up team returned home, the owner of the church pew plant reported that the operators could not keep the machine running. The start-up team returned to the plant and could not find any reason why the machine could not perform as specified. They reestablished production conditions and ran the machine for three shifts. Three shutdowns and three start-ups were performed during the three shifts. The process was turned over to the operators meeting all the agreed-upon requirements.

Three days after the start-up team returned home, the owner of the church pew plant delivered the same message! The operators could not keep the machine running. The start-up team returned to the plant and found the same situation as the first return trip. They left the plant with the process meeting all the agreed-upon requirements. Three days after they returned home, the owner of the church pew plant delivered the third message of processing problems. Something was very wrong! The president of the consulting firm came along on the next trip to the plant.

As the start-up team was going through its troubleshooting process, the president was taking a coffee break in the plant cafeteria and spotted something on a bulletin board that solved the mystery. He went out to the production floor and instructed the start-up team to shut down the process, pack up the equipment, and ship it home. He met with the owner of the plant and told him that his notice on the cafeteria bulletin board made it impossible for the new machine to ever work in his plant.

<u>ATTENTION ALL EMPLOYEES</u>

In approximately nine months a new manufacturing process will be installed that will...

- Improve quality
- Shorten the production cycle
- Ultimately eliminate multiple shifts and overtime

The employees had become used to the overtime pay, approximately 20 percent of each paycheck, and were not about to help the new process take that away. If the plant owner had set up the new process in a pilot location away from the plant and staffed it with employees from outside of the current plant population, he could have gradually made the transition from old to new technology in a rational manner.

An appropriate settlement regarding project expenses was ultimately agreed upon with some legal help.

The medical products division of a global health-care corporation had a product development project in progress to increase the range of its intravenous (IV) catheter line with the introduction of a pediatric IV catheter. The project was about 50 percent complete when the VP of the division returned from a meeting with the president to inform the project manager that they must move up the completion date by six months. The most important part of any product development project is the validation of the product design and the manufacturing process. This requires that the critical dimensions of each component be produced at the extremes of the specified tolerances. A full range of component combinations is used to manufacture samples for product testing using typical variations of manufacturing process parameters (i.e., speed, pressure, temperature, humidity, time, etc.).

In order to move up the completion date by six months, only nominal values for critical dimensions and typical manufacturing process conditions used for similar sizes in the product line were used to produce samples for validation testing. Tolerance extremes (i.e., component parts and manufacturing process parameters) were not considered. Validation testing did not raise any red flags, and the project was completed on time.

During the first production run on the manufacturing floor, everything went wrong. Not all components could be assembled. Those that got assembled could not be joined by the RF welding parameters specified. Investigations revealed that:

- Component vendors met specifications but values clustered around the high and low limits, which were not validated.

- Process parameters were set as specified, but the smaller sizes of the pediatric catheter components could not be handled at the tolerances extremes, which were not validated.

A major health-care corporation had many companies spread around the world. Each company manufactured a high-volume product to a specific market segment and supported a research and development effort to expand that market segment. In the past, when a research and development project resulted in a product that demonstrated significant sales-growth potential, a new company might be created.

At one company, the primary market segment was disposable medical devices. A disposable medical device R&D effort was in progress to add a premium urinary drainage catheter to expand the basic latex catheter capacity that had been purchased from a catheter supply house. The premium catheter consisted of a silicone body and a urethane balloon material. Laboratory test results were promising, and samples for clinical testing were being fabricated.

The marketing department projected that a successful clinical test would make its catheter line competitive with the current market leader, and the disposable catheter line would become a new spin-off company, resulting in new high-paying titles, executive perks, etc.

As the clinical samples were being prepared, a review of prior test results by QA and engineering revealed that all prior testing was done in a water environment. A urinary drainage catheter lives in human urine! Additional review of the business plan revealed that estimated first-year sales for the premier catheter were 100 percent of the total market. When senior management was informed that no testing was done in urine and first-year sales were assumed to be 100 percent of the total market share, the marketing department was dissolved.

Eventually a premium catheter was tested in urine and a clinical trial conducted. The results did not indicate a significant performance difference between the market leader and the in-house premium catheters. The expansion of the catheter business was terminated!

A small business designs and manufactures recreational products, such as pool tables, ping pong tables, and above-ground swimming pools. The pool-table line has a range of table-top thicknesses made from compressed particle board. One production line is used to produce all of the pool-table design variations. Several steel-leveling devices are screwed to the bottom of the table top to correct for variations in the table tops' flatness. Each table-top thickness requires a different length of screw to ensure a solid table/leveler connection. Thick tops require longer screws.

After the required pocket openings are cut into the top, the fabric is attached, and the table top is placed on the assembly line, fabric side up. Side and end panels are attached, and fabric-covered rubber rails are attached to the side and end panels. After attaching the corners, the table is flipped over in order to attach the steel-leveling devices. The table is then packaged and moved into the warehouse to await shipping.

One day a production run of the table with the thickest top was not completed by the end of the shift and had to be continued on the next day. The production run was completed and was followed by a number of orders for tables with thinner tops. About a week later, a complaint was received for screws sticking through the table tops.

The hunt for the root cause of the problem revealed that the longer screws from the production run for thicker top tables were not removed from the assembly line when the run was completed. Since the table top is not inspected after it is flipped bottom up to attach the leveling devices, there was no opportunity to catch the mistake.

A global medical-products company was always dealing with project plan conflicts. The divisions of the company consisted of finance, sales and marketing, research and development, technical operations, and quality assurance/control. The president's staff developed a list of the top ten projects that were critical to the company's growth. The president created a middle management task force to look into the project planning problem. Task force results revealed that there was no agreement between the divisions regarding the top ten projects, and the company's resources were only capable of working on two projects at any given time!

The conclusion was that the goals of upper management were not clearly communicated to the organization. Each division worked on its own priority list, and there was no formal project planning process in place.

Historical Engineering Disasters

- Hyatt Hotel (1981)
- Titanic (1912)
- Teton Dam (1976)
- Aloha Airlines Flight 243 (1988)
- TWA Flight 800 (1996)
- Apollo test fire (1967)
- Apollo 13 (1970)
- Challenger (1986)
- Hubble Space Telescope (1990)
- Three Mile Island (1979)
- Chernobyl (1986)
- Bhopal India (1984)
- Chauchat Machine Gun (1917)
- Thresher Submarine (1963)
- Liberty Ships (WW II)
- The Andrea Doria (1956)
- Hartford Civic Center (1978)
- Kemper Arena (1979)
- Saint Francis Dam (1928)
- Northeast Blackout (1965)

Appendix D

Education in Finland

The list of countries that might qualify as a benchmark for education is short. Finland is at the top of that list because four of their operating philosophies capture the essence of common sense.

- ► Children are the most important resource that a country can have.

- ► A superbly educated workforce has a major impact on the development of a country's economy.

- ► The natural potential of each student must be fully developed.

- ► The difference between the best student and the worst student must be minimized.

Finland and America have the same type of government: presidential and republic. In Finland all parties on the right and left agree that the most important resource of a nation is its people and that equality is the most important word in Finish education.

- ► People in the government agencies running the school system, from national officials to local authorities, are educators, not business people, military leaders, or career politicians.

- ► There is a national curriculum.

- ► Every school, public and private, has the same national goals and draws from the same pool of university-trained educators.

- Teaching is a high-status profession.

- The curriculum for a teaching degree is the most comprehensive and rigorous of any professional career.

- Professionals are selected from the top 10 percent of the nation's graduates to earn the required master's degree in education. Teachers must have a master's degree!

- Finland's education system has no tuition fees, and fully subsidized meals are served to full-time students. The education system consists of:

  ▷ Daycare programs for infants and toddlers.

  ▷ One-year pre-school or kindergarten for six-year-olds.

  ▷ Nine-year compulsory basic comprehensive school starting at age seven.

  ▷ Post-compulsory secondary general academic and vocational education.

  ▷ Higher education — university and university of applied sciences.

  ▷ Adult (i.e., lifelong, continuing) education.

- Finland has a comprehensive preschool program that emphasizes self-reflection and socializing, not academics.

- Students have light homework loads.

- Finish schools do not have classes for gifted students.

- Finland uses very little standard testing.

- Students are separated into academic and vocational tracks during the last three years of high school. Approximately 50 percent go into each track.

- Diagnostic testing of students is used early and frequently. If a student is in need of extra help, intensive intervention is provided.

▶ Groups of teachers visit each other's classes to observe their colleagues at work. Teachers also get one afternoon per week for professional development.

▶ School funding is higher for the middle school years, the years when children are most in danger of dropping out.

▶ Grades are not given until high school, and even then class rankings are not compiled.

▶ Teachers in Finland spend fewer hours at school each day and spend less time in classrooms than American teachers. Teachers use the extra time to build curriculums and assess their students.

▶ Children spend far more time playing outside, even in the depths of winter.

▶ It is almost unheard of for a child to show up hungry or homeless.

▶ Finland provides three years of maternity leave and subsidized day care to parents, and preschool for all five-year-olds, where the emphasis is on play and socializing.

▶ The state subsidizes parents, paying them a monthly stipend for every child until he or she turns seventeen.

▶ Ninety-seven percent of six-year-olds attend public preschool, where children begin some academics.

▶ Schools provide food, medical care, counseling, and transportation if needed.

▶ Student health care is free.

Appendix E

References, Assumptions & Calculations

Cost Estimates

Universal Free Health Care

Bernie and the high cost of "free" health care/New York Post
(https://nypost.com/2016/01/31bernie-and-the-high-cost-of-free-health-care/)

Roughly $13.8 trillion over its first decade of operation.

Roughly $1.38 trillion per year

Use $1.4 trillion

Universal Free Education

https://www.npr.org/...hillary's-free-tution-promise-what-would-it-cost-how-would-it...

Sanders campaign estimate
College: $75 billion
https://nces.ed.gov/fastfacts/display_asp?id=66
U.S. spending for K-12 for 2013-2014 = $634 billion
College + K-12 = $75 billion + $634 billion = $709 billion.
Use $.709 trillion

The New American Foundation recommended a five-year, $1.2 trillion investment program ($0.24 trillion per year), saying, "It is estimated that every $1 billion of public infrastructure investment generates, by the most conservative estimates, 23,000 well-paying jobs." The authors of the report said their recommendations, if fully implemented, would create 5.2 million jobs in each of the program's five years. Beyond this, they said, "It is important to note that infrastructure investment has a healthy multiplier effect throughout the economy. The CBO (Congressional Budget Office) estimates that every dollar of infrastructure spending generates on average a $1.6 increase in GDP (Gross Domestic Product). Some critical transportation and energy projects have even larger multiplier effects." America will not be able to get its economic act together without a major, long-term commitment to rebuild its physical plant.

Use $1 trillion per year

That is the aggressive investment program needed.

The approximate total cost of the programs presented above is $3.11 trillion for the first year of operation.

Universal free health care . . . .$1.4 trillion
Universal free education . . . .$.709 trillion
Infrastructure . . . .$1 trillion

Alternate Sources of Funding

1% TAX ON CURRENCY TRADED

https://www.fxcm.com/uk/forex/what-is-forex/

FX, or currency trading, is a decentralized global market where the entire world's currency is traded. The forex market is the largest, most liquid market in the world, with an average daily trading volume exceeding $5 trillion.

htpp://forexsystemprofits.com/how-many-forex-trading-days-in-a-year/

There are 286 trading days per year.

https://en.wikipedia.org/wiki/Forien_exchange_market#Market_participants

Five U.S. banks account for 36 percent of daily trading volume.

Daily U.S. trading volume = .36 * $5 trillion = $1.8 trillion.

Yearly U.S. trading volume = 286 * $1.8 trillion = $514.8 trillion

1% tax = $5.148 trillion

REDUCTION OF MEDICARE FRAUD

http://www.klf.org/medicare/issue-brief/the-facts-on-medicare-spending-and-financing.

2016 Medicare Spending + Medicaid Spending = $.98 trillion

https://www.forbes.com/sites/merrillmatthews/2012/05/31/medicare-and-medicaid-fraud-is-costing-taxpayers-billions/#29b4cld57331

Assume Fraud = 40 percent

Fraud = .40 * .98 trillion $.392 trillion

Assume a 50/50 program of fraud reduction (i.e., government and the individual or group identifying the fraud share the savings, tax-free).

Government share = .50 * 0.392 trillion = $.196 trillion

1% TAX ON TOTAL BANK ASSETS

https://www.statista.com/statistics/250005/largest-banks-in-the-united states-by—total-assets/

2017 = $13,138.24 billion for the top 15

1% tax = $131,382,400,000

INCREASED EFFICIENCY OF FEDERAL WORKFORCE

http://www.businessinsider.com

"Over the course of an eight-hour workday, the average employee works for about three hours — two hours and 53 minutes, to be more precise."

Assume 40 percent of actual work during an eight–hour day.

Congressional Research Service, Table 3.

2017 Estimate = 2,800,000 civilian employees

U.S. Office of Personnel Management

The average yearly salary for pay grade GS-8 is approximately $43,300.

http://money.cnn.com/2013/02/28/smallbusiness/salary-benefits/index.html

The actual cost of an employee is 20 percent added to his or her salary. Therefore, the actual cost of a GS-8 employee is approximately $53,000 per year.

If employee efficiency is increased from 40 percent to 60 percent, and the amount of work required remains constant, the number of employees required is decreased.

2.8 million * 0.40 = x * 0.60

x = the number of employees at 60 percent efficiency

x = 1.7 million employees

The number of employees saved = 2.8 million – 1.7 million = 1.1 million

$ Savings = 1.1 million * $53,000 = $58,300,000,000

1% TAX ON INSURANCE COMPANY ASSETS

https://www.statista.com/statistics/431580/leading-insurance-companies-usa-by-total-assets/

2016 = $4,416.410 billion

1% tax = $44,164,100,000

1% Tax on Imports

https://wits.worldbank.org/countrysnapshot/USA/textview

2016 = $2,248,209 million

1% tax = $22,482,090,000

Quarterly National 50/50 Raffles — Tax-free

http://money.cnn.com/2015/02/11/news/companies/lottery-spending/index.html

In 2014 Americans spent a total of $70 billion on lottery tickets.

Assume that the lure of a tax-free prize would result in the national raffles getting 50 percent of the $70 billion sales for standard lottery tickets, or $35 billion.

A 50/50 split would yield the government $17.5 billion.

1% Tax on Exports

https://wits.worldbank.org/countrysnapshot/USA/textview

2016 = $1,450,457 million

1% tax = $14,504,570,000

1% Tax on Entertainment & Media Revenue

https://selectusa.gov/media-entertainment-industry-united-states

2021 forecast = $804 billion

1% tax = $8,040,000,000

1% Tax on Gas & Oil Revenue

https://www.statista.com/statistics/257417/top-10-oil-and-gas-companies-worldwide-based-on-revenue/

2017 = $683.29 billion for the top 10

1% tax = $6,832,900,000

1% Tax on Amazon U.S. Revenue

https://www.statista.com/statistics/266282/annual-net-revenue-of-amazoncom/

2017 = $365.2 billion

1% tax = $3,652,000,000

1% Tax on Pharmaceutical Revenue

https://statista.com/statistics/233971/top-25-pharmaceutical-corporations-by-us-sales/

2016 = $337.3 billion for the top 20

1% tax = $3,373,000,000

1% Tax on Alcoholic Beverages

https://www.statista.com/statistics/207936/us-total-alcoholic-beverages-sales-since-1990/

2016 = $223.2 billion

1% tax = $2,232,000,000

1% TAX ON AIRLINE REVENUE

https://learn.stashinvest.com/us-airlines-by-revenue

2017 = $158.2 billion

1% tax = $1,582,000,000

1% TAX ON TOBACCO REVENUE

https://www.statista.com/statistics/4917091/tobacco-united-states-market-value/

2017 = $121,226.8 million

1% tax = $1,212,268,000

1% TAX ON PENTAGON WAR SPENDING

http://www.newsweek.com/war-spending-flint-healthcare-college-puerto-rico-poverty-702591

Over a period of sixteen years, the Pentagon spent an average of $250 million per day.

2017 war spending = $250 million x 365 days per year = $91,250,000,000
1% tax = $912,500,000

1% TAX ON CASINO GAMBLING

https://www.statista.com/statistics/271583/casino-gaming-market-in-the-us/

2016 U.S. casino revenue = $73.1 billion

1% tax = $731,000,000

1% Tax on U.S. Professional Sports League Revenue

https://ipfs.io/ipfs/QmXoypizjW3WknFiJnKLwHCnL72vedxjQkDDP1mX
Wo6uco/wiki/List_of_professional_sports_leagues_by_revenue.html

2014–2015 = $36,141.04 million

1% tax = $361,410,400

Tax on Shares Traded, (0.01) $/Share

https://en.wikipedia.org/wiki/Trading_day

Average number of trading days = 252 days per year.

https://www.itg.com/trading-volume/quarter/

First three quarters of 2017 — average shares traded per day = 141,203,045.

2017 total shares traded = 252 x 141,203,045 = 35,583,167,340.

(0.01)$/Share tax = $355,831,673

1% Tax on Local TV Revenue

http://www.broadcastingcable.com/news/currency/study-tv-station-revenue-reach-326-billion-2020/165050

2020 forecast = $32.78 billion

1% tax = $327,800,000

1% Tax on Amusement Park Revenue

https://fred.stlouisfed.org/series/REVEF7131/TAXABL

2014 = $14,600 million

1% tax = $146,000,000

1% TAX ON GUN & AMMO REVENUE

https://www.cnbc.com/2015/10/02/americas-gun-business-by-the-numbers.html

2015 = $13.5 billion

1% tax = $135,000,000

1% TAX ON PRIVATE PRISON REVENUE

http://nique.net/options/2017/03/31/profits-are-king-in-private-prison-industry/

2015 = $3.68 billion for the top 2

1% tax = $36,800,000

Appendix F

20?? Budget / Funding

https://www.usgovernmentspending.com/federal_budget_estimate_vs_actual_2017

https://www.treasurydirect.gov/govt/reports/ir/ir_expense.htm

https://en.wikipedia.org/wiki/Social_Security_debate_in_the_United_States#
Social_Security_Trust_Fund

Budget	$ trillion	% of bud
• Universal Free Health Care (New Paradigm)	1.40	15.6
• Universal Free Education (New Paradigm)	0.75	8.3
• Infrastructure (New Paradigm)	1.00	11.1
• Social Security (double the 2016 actual)	1.55	17.2
• Defense/Protection (2017 actual)	0.86	9.6
• Debt Interest Payment (double the 2017 actual)	0.92	10.2
• Pensions (2017 actual)	1.01	11.2
• Science (New Paradigm: 2015 was 1% of budget)	0.50	5.6
• Environment/Energy (New Paradigm: 2015 was 1% of budget)	0.50	5.6
• Welfare (2017 actual)	0.36	4.0
• General Government/Transportation (2017 actual)	0.14	1.6
Total	8.99	100.0

- Doubling the Social Security entry increases the strength and safety of the program.

- Doubling the debt interest payment creates additional funds for debt reduction.

- The format for the federal budget needs to be formalized to facilitate year-to-year comparisons.

Funding

Funding will be supplied from the list of Alternate Sources of Funding presented in pages above.

A net 1 percent model results in $5,407,963,670,073 of funding.

A net 2 percent model results in $10,815,927,340,146 of funding.

A net 3 percent model results in $16,223,891,010,219 of funding.

Using the net 2 percent model results in an excess of $1,825,927,340,146, which could be used for debt reduction. Since the budget already contains an extra debt payment of $0.460 trillion, the total amount available for debt reduction would be $1.826 + 0.460 = $2.286 trillion.

Many other models are possible if we think "outside the box."